Lords of Creation

A Play for Young People

John Wiles

A SAMUEL FRENCH ACTING EDITION

FOUNDED 1830

SAMUELFRENCH-LONDON.CO.UK
SAMUELFRENCH.COM

FOR AMATEUR PRODUCTION ENQUIRIES

UNITED KINGDOM AND WORLD EXCLUDING NORTH AMERICA

plays@SamuelFrench-London.co.uk

020 7255 4302/01

Each title is subject to availability from Samuel French,

depending upon country of performance.

CHARACTERS

Lords of Creation was originally presented at the
Cockpit (ILEA) Theatre in London. This revised
version was first staged by the Scottish Youth Theatre
in Edinburgh. Both productions were by the author.

Storyteller
Drummers
Dancers
Chamberlain
Tangaroa
Cheeky Boy
Shy One, Loud One, Abrupt, Accurate, Accusing, Adenoi-
dal, Affable, Affected, Aggressive, Anxious, Arrogant,
Bass, Squeaky, Bewildered, Blasé, Blithe, Boastful,
Boisterous, Bold, Bombastic, Bookish, Curious, Excited,
Motherly, Logical
1st, 2nd, 3rd, 4th Wise Ones
Recorder
Neighbour
1st, 2nd, 3rd, 4th, 5th Clerks
Moja
Lioness
1st, 2nd, 3rd Cubs
1st, 2nd, 3rd, 4th Assistant Storytellers
Stump Tooth
Jackal
Devil-lion
Rajah, the Elephant
Vedda, the mahout
Humming-bird
Orca, the Whale
Sailors
Donkey
Messenger
Human
Aquila, the Eagle
Monkeys
Philosopher
Astro-physicist
Eicke

1st, 2nd, 3rd Black Figures/Nucleus
Yama-Hiko
Ontake-San

The above is a list of the characters who appear in the play. Some of these are non-speaking or have only one line so much doubling is possible.

The action of the play takes place in a jungle clearing.

AUTHOR'S NOTE

The present version of *Lords of Creation* was written for a multi-ethnic cast of about 75; nevertheless all but ten of these parts can be doubled, tripled or even quadrupled. On the other hand if a larger cast hast to be catered for, a number of roles can be divided up. For example, the role of the Storyteller has been shared successfully between a girl and a boy and may very well succeed better that way.

The story is presented in the form of a Balinese folk-tale, but the exact location is unspecified. The main action takes place in a jungle clearing and this can be as elaborate or as simple as the designer wishes or as local conditions dictate.

Finally, there is no music score to accompany this text. In the initial productions both musical directors—Peter Somerville in London and Bernard Shaw in Scotland—encouraged the cast to make their own Oriental music with the aid of finger xylophones, gongs of various sizes and bells. May I urge that this is always more exciting and productive than using pre-recorded commercial tapes.

J. W.

BEFORE THE PLAY

When the audience comes in, the cast is already on the stage limbering up. The exercises they do should be those they have used during preliminary drama classes and should include loosening up the muscles of the limbs, of the face and torso, stretching the spine, revolving the head and so on. All this work should be done in silence and either under supervision of one of their number or (preferably) with each member of the cast working quietly in his or her own way.

All care should be taken to avoid any sign of "panic". The audience should not feel that something has gone wrong, but be encouraged to sit and watch what is going on. The "show" has, in fact, started. the actors can be wearing basic costumes or colourful rehearsal gear, but whatever the clothing, the effect should be that of *hard work*.

A quarter of an hour before the advertised time of starting, the Stage Manager should announce—either in person or over the tannoy—"Fifteen minutes, please". Now a new air of drama creeps into the preparations, but this is offset by the impression of control and discipline coming from the stage where the members of the company are engaged on relaxation exercises. "Ten minutes, please, ten minutes", increases the feeling of countdown. Some of the cast get up from the floor and leave the stage to prepare their costumes and make-up. Others continue to work. The Stage Manager passes quietly amongst them, giving last minute instructions in a calm, quiet voice. Once again it is important to assure the audience that all this is *intended*.

At the ten-minute call, a new effect can be added. Out of sight an orchestra can be heard tuning up. Perhaps behind the preparation noises we also hear the murmur and excitement of a large and expectant audience.

"Five minutes, five minutes, please." More of the cast leave. Those who are left work harder, don't rush, don't play for laughs, show no awareness of the audience at all, but build up the air of anticipation. The sounds of the orchestra grow louder. The countdown is approaching H-Hour now.

"Beginners, beginners, please." The stage is almost empty. One or two boys and girls are hanging on until the last moment, but finally even they gather up their sweaters and towels and dart from the stage. A pause. One small boy races back to collect his jacket.

M-Minute. the orchestra breaks off. Silence. Loud applause as the invisible conductor takes his place and in the pause before the overture starts—the house lights go down.

ACT I*

Five big crashes on an Oriental drum. Instantly the theatre is filled with the sound of tropical birds of every kind, shrieking, calling, chattering

The Lights come up to reveal the Storyteller in the centre of the acting area. He is bare-chested and bare-footed and wears a colourful sarong tucked in at the waist. He is standing with feet planted firmly apart and bows to the audience from the hips with the palms of his hands resting on his knees. Then he straightens up, looks around him and addresses the birds

Storyteller Be quiet!

The birds continue

Where are your manners? (*Louder*) Be quiet!!

The birds continue. A thought strikes him. He says in a more controlled manner

Be quiet ... please.

The birds break off obediently. He smiles and sits comfortably

When you come right down to it, we are all children of one god or another. Even those who don't believe, make a kind of religion of their disbelief. The name of this deity is unimportant. Call him Akna, Jehova, Mazda, Allah, even the Universal Sub-Conscious ... it is all one to me. (*He settles himself more comfortably and smiles*) Our god is called Tangaroa—you'll see him in a moment. But above him is an even greater god whom we call simply ... God. One day—so the story goes—this ... "God" sent for Tangaroa and said, "I've decided all this must go. The mountains, the forests, the oceans—even the very fish that live in the oceans. Find me half a dozen species that deserve to survive. All the rest must perish." "But, Tuan, great God." Tangaroa said, "how am I to find six species more deserving than the rest?" "Hold a contest," God said. "The details I leave to you." And he mounted his chariot of fire and rode away. Poor Tangaroa. What a responsibility. Six species out of all this! Well, he did his best. The contest was announced and from far and wide the species came: on four feet and two and on a hundred; on wing and belly and paw; by sea and air—some floated on leaves!—and through the very bowels of the earth. Some could not come but sent messages— "Great Tangaroa, I am anchored by my giant roots and have been so for a thousand years. Please hear my plea." Poor Tanga, he wept. Who would

---

*N.B. Paragraph 3 on page ii of this Acting Edition regarding photocopying and video-recording should be carefully read.

lightly kill a giant mango just because he could not present his appeal in tree-person? (*Comfortably*) This place is called the stomach of the earth. Up there is our volcano called Gunung Agung which means the Navel of the World. (*Airily*) We are very sophisticated, you see. Well, to this Navel came everything crawling, galloping, squirming (*he shudders*) very nasty some of them . . . hopping, whirring, snapping and grunting. What a . . . GIANT . . . concourse! And each in turn convinced that he and he alone was worth the saving. Poor Tanga. The first round took forty years alone and that only whittled them down to fifty thousand. "Ai . . . ai . . . ai," said our little god, "at this rate we'll be here all eternity and I'll never get the job done." "You'd better," said Tuan God, "The Great Destruction will follow in exactly one hundred years and if you haven't chosen six by then—*everything* will go." Such a panic! Such a—whirring, grunting, snarling, roaring, chirping, snapping, barking, you couldn't hear yourself think! But fifty thousand became a thousand, a thousand became a hundred, a hundred became fifty, and fifty became twelve. There is a saying in Africa—"The last Wednesday of the month is unlucky for any undertaking." (*He tries it*) *Ni ukorifi Kufanya* . . . I'm sorry, my Swahili isn't very good. Well, we've reached the last Wednesday of the last month of the hundred years and it's certainly going to be unlucky for some.

The Drummers have entered. He exchanges a nod with them

Here comes Tangaroa now to begin the last selection. (*He rises and bows as before*) This is my tale. Let it come from me to you!

The Drummers start: a fast, trotting rhythm in the manner of the Japanese Zaondekoza drummers. The sounds of the birds return and the Lights come up fully to show us a clearing in the forest

The Temple Dancers enter on all levels—boys as well as girls—some with gongs, finger-bells or wooden clackers. Stamping, twisting, using hand—and head—movements, uplifted "sickle" feet, they process around the acting area. All are dressed in sarongs and wear necklaces and bangles and ankle bracelets which chime and tinkle as they move. All are barefooted and move their feet in time to the beat of the drums. Faster, faster, faster—the whole stage should blaze with colour and movement

Now follows the Chamberlain more elaborately dressed and walking backwards, staff in hand and bowing, bowing low as Tangaroa enters, borne on a palanquin carried by some of the boys. (This palanquin can be stripped to form a simple raft.) The god can wear Oriental robes or else be barechested; the single status symbol he or she should wear is the god-mask, chunkily carved with boar's tusks or horns, snarling mouth, fearsomely painted eyes and frowning brows

What else? Yes, the Chamberlain (if possible) should wear a wig of flowing white hair that reaches his shoulders and all bodies should be browned, make-up being kept to the minimum (eyes slanted in the Oriental fashion is all that is required) and the girls' hair should be loose. If we seek any geographical location at all, it should be that of South-east Asia. Now the palanquin is set down, the god ascends his throne—a block of stone—the Chamberlain commands silence and all fall to the earth and grovel in obeisance, not in fear, for Tanga is a popular god, but in respect. Out of the silence—even the birds are hushed—the flute introduces a simple melodic line punctuated by heavy blows on the largest drum. The Chamberlain vocalizes about the beginning of the world

Chamberlain   When my lord breathes . . .
                    When my lord sees . . .
                    He is like a corpse . . .
                    Like a lone corpse . . .
                    Here in the ground.

                    But when he breathes,
                    When he sees,
                    When he frowns,
                    The world shakes
                    As it is shaking now.

The drums grow faster

(Chanting quickly) In the middle of the world, there was nothing but sea and above the sea where the sky should be, was the Old-Spider.
All The Old-Spider.
Chamberlain One day the Spider found on the ground a giant clam bigger than this earth, bigger, bigger . . .
All Bigger, bigger . . .
Chamberlain She held the clam to her ear. "What is this? What is here?" How to find a way inside? She tapped on it. It was hollow, hollow . . .
All Hollow, hollow . . .
Chamberlain So she took a snail and said, "Open this clam that I can get inside." The snail did. Inch by inch the clam was opened.
All Glory! glory!
Chamberlain The upper half became the sky, the lower half the earth. The snail, exhausted by all its labours, died.
All Poor snail!
Chamberlain But the Old-Spider took a second snail and made the sun of it. *(Off-hand)* And that is how the world was made.
All Well! well! well!

The drums grow louder. The Storyteller steps forward

Storyteller There are other versions, of course. Once upon a time everything was covered with fog and Raki, which is Heaven, said to Papa, which is Earth, "Make all manner of things which live and breathe and move." And Papa took the fog——

The drums have grown too loud. The Storyteller shrugs and gives up. The Drummers compete, exhorting each other with cries of "Now!" "Faster!" "There!" After a while the sound fades in intensity but keeps going in the background

(*Trying again*) Others explain it differently. Some say the earth came out of the sea, or from a rock in the sea, or that a deity took six days to make it and then rested on the seventh—whoever heard of a god needing a rest!—and others that it was no more than a piece of fluff from his navel which he fashioned into a ball (*as if by magic he produces a golden ball*) spins and spins and spins . . . and flies through the air from god to god——

He throws it to this one and that of the others who are sitting now and they toss it back and forth as he speaks

—back and forth, to and fro. (*The ball is thrown back to him and he points out an invisible spot on it*) And here we are, this tiny, tiny place. But tiny as it is, the whole world knows it revolves around this place.

The drums come up louder again. The Chamberlain waves the Storyteller away impatiently

Chamberlain Tangaroa is our Lord, eater of the stars, consumer of the seas. All hail to Tangaroa!
All All hail! (*They do obeisance again*)

The drums stop with a crash. Out of the silence:

Storyteller In other parts of the world they tell us, some people worship (*carefully*) "the mo-tor-car" or "the jet-plane" and "the tran-sis-tor". Foolish people. We worship Tangaroa and we know we are right because he has told us so. Such a shame all peoples are not as sophisticated as we.
Chamberlain Quiet! The god would speak.

The Storyteller glares at him. The Chamberlain corrects himself

Quiet . . . *please.*

The Storyteller bows and steps back. They all wait

Tangaroa B-b-b-b——
Storyteller (*aside, a whisper*) I didn't tell you our god suffers from a tiny impediment. It is a most *divine* affliction.
Tangaroa D-d-d-d——
Chamberlain (*helpfully*) Dog?
Cheeky Boy Sing it!

A crash of thunder, a flash of lightning and the Cheeky Boy screams and rolls over in agony

Storyteller (*smugly*) It doesn't pay to joke with the gods.
Tangaroa M-m-m-m——
Chamberlain (*nodding*) I understand completely. The god wishes to know the names of all the species rejected in the last round.
Storyteller (*deeply impressed*) You have to have very special training to be able to understand the god so *well!*
Chamberlain Begin!
Shy One The aardvark and the aasvogel!

Chamberlain Speak up!
Shy One The aardvark and the aasvogel!
Chamberlain Which were they?
Storyteller The South African anteater and vulture.
Chamberlain (*worried*) I hope we won't be accused of discrimination. (*Loudly*) Next!
Loud One The acacia. (*Helpfully*) That's a tree of the mimosa tribe.
Chamberlain (*testily*) I know what an *acacia* is. Go on, go on!
Abrupt One The addax.
Accurate The adder.
Accusing The agama.
Adenoidal The agami.
Chamberlain No, no, no, she's just said that.
Storyteller Yes, yes, yes. The first is an Indian lizard, the second an American bird.
Chamberlain (*roaring*) QUIET! (*A gesture to continue*)
Affable The aigrette.
Affected The airedale . . . Hairedale.
Aggressive The albacare!
Anxious The albatross . . . I think.
Chamberlain What do you mean, you think? Either we rejected it or we did not!
Anxious Yes, we did. (*Bravely, louder*) The albatross!

The others applaud politely

Arrogant The alder, almond, aloe . . .
Bass Alpaca, alsatian, amaryllis . . .
Squeaky Anaconda, anchusa, anemone . . .
Bewildered What? Oh, yes . . . the angora, antelope, antirrhinum. . .(*To Squeaky*) Was that right?
Blasé Aphis, apple, apricot . . .
Blithe Areca, argala, argali . . .
Chamberlain (*despairing*) Here we go again!
Storyteller The one's a stork, the other's a wild sheep.
Chamberlain A wild SHEEP?
Boastful Armadillo, artichoke, arum . . .
Boisterous Ash, asp, aspen . . .
Bold Asphodel, aubergine, auk . . .
Bombastic Auricula, avocado, aye-aye . . .
Chamberlain Aye-aye?
Bombastic It's a Madagascan cat.
Chamberlain ENOUGH! The god has heard ENOUGH!
Storyteller (*to the audience*) And that was only the As. Think how long it would have taken if we'd gone through the alphabet! (*To the Bookish One*) How many have been rejected since the beginning of the year?
Bookish (*consulting her records*) Seven hundred and forty-one.
Storyteller So you see what a difficult task faces the god! To come, twelve — from which he must select six. (*Sadly*) Ai . . . ai . . . ai . . . ai . . . ai.

Bombastic That's two-and-a-half Madagascan cats.
Chamberlain SILENCE! My lord's selection committee is now in session.

Music. A slow ritualistic dance takes the actors into new groups. While it is going on, the Storyteller explains

Storyteller To assist him in his task, the god has appointed a panel of experts called the Wise Ones. (*Airily*) They know everything about everything. What makes the sun hot, what makes water wet, what makes the night dark—all that sort of thing.
Curious What does make the night dark?
Storyteller The sun is sleeping, of course.
Curious Ah . . .
Storyteller And if she cannot see us, how can we see her? Now pay attention, please. The hearings are about to begin.

The Lights begin to narrow down until only the central area is lit. During the above we have seen the Court arranging itself with the Wise Ones taking their places on either side of Tangaroa and the Chamberlain's staff preparing their lists. One has the task of keeping the records by chiselling marks on a stone. Not surprisingly events always happen too fast for him

Recorder (*the stone-cutter*) What's the date?
3rd Clerk The twenty-first day after the Spring moon.
Recorder Thank you. (*He starts to chip at the stone*)
Chamberlain First candidate for survival—the lion!
1st Clerk The lion!
2nd Clerk The lion!
3rd Clerk (*sleepy*) Oh, not him again. The lion! Ho-hum . . .
4th Clerk The lion!
Recorder How do you spell that?

4th Clerk shows him

5th Clerk The lion!
Storyteller (*to the audience*) We love ritual, you see.

The cry of "The lion!" is carried back into the wings

   The Lion's party enter carrying their masks under their arms in the manner of warriors. They bow to the Court, don their masks, and take up their ritualistic starting positions. The music starts—gongs and bells. The Lions' Dance is one of catlike movements, stealthy but strong. They prowl . . . pounce . . . stretch . . . wash their faces with their paws . . . rear proudly . . . sleep deeply . . . wake instantly

The spectators sway in time to the rhythm and make polite comments of appreciation. At the end of the dance, the music stops, the dancers hold their positions, and Moja steps forward. He tosses his mane proudly and flails with his paws

Moja I am Lion!

Spectators (*separately*) Yes, you can see that ... isn't he handsome ... I hope he's not too fierce ... *etc.*
Lioness (*rather bored*) I'm his mate.
Moja I am the King of the Beasts.
Lioness I'm his female.
Moja I strike terror into all who behold me.
Lioness Except me. I hunt for him, kill for him, bear his cubs and look after the family.
Cubs (*squeaky*) We're the family! (*They try to walk and fall over*)

The Lioness hauls them to their feet

Lioness The sooner you learn to walk the better.
Moja My story concerns Devil-beast, the greatest lion of them all. And how I defeated him.

Murmurs of excitement from the spectators

Lioness (*to the cubs*) Take your positions, and don't fall over.

Moja waves an imperious paw at the Storyteller's 1st Assistant

Moja Begin.
1st Assistant Very well. In the country of the Serengeti near the place known as Mamoto in the land of the two-leggeds called the Baganda, there lived a whole colony of lions ruled over by the King Moja.

The Lights come up very hot and dry

Moja I am Moja. It means Number One. I am King Number One of all the lions of the Serengeti. All who hear my roar, tremble!
Lioness Except me.
1st Assistant More than one hundred square miles belonged to this Moja. While his female hunted and protected the cubs, he patrolled his kingdom ceaselessly in the company of Stump Tooth, his aged deputy, to keep out intruders.

Moja and Stump Tooth prowl. The Lioness moves between the cubs, always watching, always expecting trouble. Moja and his friend reach a high point and there settle to survey the landscape and snuffle at the dust

Moja I tell you, Stump Tooth, I often wonder if in the whole universe of lions, I am not the greatest of them all.

Stump Tooth gives a non-commital grunt

Who else has a kingdom so wide, so long and so full of Thompson gazelles to please the stomach?

Stump Tooth gives another low growl

Well, speak up. Don't just lie there clearing your throat.
1st Assistant Now Stump Tooth was no fool. He didn't want to contradict Moja, you see, but he had heard, well, he had heard—well, you'll hear what he had heard.

Stump Tooth I think you're right to be proud, Moja. Your kingdom certainly is a glory to behold. Nevertheless, well . . .

Moja (*sharply*) Nevertheless, what? Speak up!

Stump Tooth I have heard that over to the East there does live a beast so powerful, so menacing that when he shakes his mane the whole earth grows dark. And as for his roar . . .

Moja What about his roar? Is it more terrible than mine?

Stump Tooth Well, they do say that when he shouts, the trees sway, the corn bows down and bolts of light come from the sky.

Moja Impossible. The lion who can make trees dance has never been invented, although I dare say I come pretty close to it.

Stump Tooth Well . . . if you say so . . .

Moja Of course I say so. Anyway, show me his face. Can any face be as handsome as mine?

Stump Tooth (*worried*) Nobody's seen his face, that's half the trouble. For whenever he appears, the sky is so full of streaks of light, you can't see anything else.

Moja (*impressed*) Simba . . .

Stump Tooth As for his claws, they do tell how one swipe is enough to flatten all the grasslands between here and the Salt Water Hole, and you know how far off that is. (*He goes on talking in mime*)

1st Assistant And the more Stump Tooth went on speaking, the more impressed Moja became. Was there ever such a threat to his kingdom, he thought.

Moja I tell you, Stump Tooth, there is only one thing to do. You must seek out this devil and kill him.

Stump Tooth I? Not on your life.

Moja Why not? You're my deputy, the Number One of the Number One, are you not?

Stump Tooth But this is no job for a deputy! If anybody's going to challenge the monster, it ought to be you.

Moja Rubbish. It's below my dignity.

1st Assistant But in his heart, Moja knew his friend was right.

Moja (*aside*) Oh, Simba, I'm afraid. What Stump Tooth has said is the truth. It certainly is my task to challenge the outsider, but what can I do? Inside I am a very small lion, although the sweep of my tail is enough to put all the animals of my kingdom to flight.

1st Assistant And while Moja lay there digesting this terrible news, and Stump Tooth kept glancing over his shoulder in case the Devil-lion had crept up on them unnoticed, the sun bounced gently in the sky and then went down the hill in search of its blanket.

The Lights go to night

Meanwhile, back at the home-cave. (*Nervously to Moja*) We haven't done this bit.

Moja Just get on.

1st Assistant Back at the home-cave . . .

1st Cub I'm hungry.

2nd Cub So am I.

3rd Cub Me too, me too!

1st Assistant I think that's right.

Lioness (*no nonsense*) Be quiet! Can't you see I'm just going out to find some food. And while I'm gone, don't take any chances. Lie very still and don't dare go outside. And don't forget to wash your feet. Remember what they say, a lion who doesn't wash his paws before going to sleep, lies down with the devil.

1st Cub I think it's a stupid expression. What's it mean, anyway?

Lioness It doesn't matter what it means, just remember it. Well, I'm off . . .

2nd Cub Can we have buffalo tonight?

3rd Cub Or a nice mongoose?

Lioness You'll have what you're given and no nonsense. (*She goes*)

The cubs watch her go and then grow restless

1st Assistant But things didn't work out like that. The eldest cub who, as you've seen, was something of a teenage rebel, hardly waited for his mother to go, before he stuck his nose out of the cave. This attracting the attention of a Back-Striped Jackal who happened to be nosing about, and——

The Jackal slips into the cave

—within a trice the cubs were dead. The youngest got as far as thinking, "perhaps we ought to have washed our paws after all", but the oldest knew it was his fault for sticking his nose outside the cave . . . anyway it was soon over and when they opened their eyes again, they were in Simba-heaven which is a place very like this, only without any of the worries.

The Jackal eats his fill and then goes

Meanwhile their mother was continuing to hunt. Torn between a wart hog, a Masai giraffe and a red duiker, she was trying to make up her mind when she was charged by a black rhinoceros and before she knew it, she was dead——

The fight is enacted as described

—and had joined her children in Simba-heaven.

Lioness (*sitting up*) What are you all doing here?

3rd Cub We didn't listen to you, Mother.

Lioness Let that be a lesson to you.

They all lie down again

Storyteller You'll notice nobody thought to ask the mother what *she'd* learnt. But that's the privilege of mothers anywhere . . .

1st Assistant Came the dawn . . .

The Lights stay down

Came the dawn . . . came the dawn . . .

Storyteller I think it's meant to be like this.

1st Assistant (*glancing at her scroll*) Ah, yes. Came the dawn, but instead of a lessening of the dark, the stars remained covered. Moja, who had spent the night travelling back to the home-cave with Stump Tooth, glanced up at the sky.

Moja I think we're in for a storm.

Stump Tooth (*nervously*) What if they're not clouds, but the flying mane of the Devil-beast?

Moja Nonsense, I'd recognize cumulo-nimbus anywhere.

A distant growl of thunder

Stump Tooth (*in a panic*) No, no, listen to that. I tell you that's his roar.

Moja Rubbish. Have you gone *bata*?

1st Assistant Bats.

Moja That's the voice of the rain-god.

Stump Tooth No, no, it's the growl of the Devil-lion.

Moja Are you sure? I could have sworn——

A giant crack of thunder, lightning and the sound of rain

Stump Tooth It is he, it is he!

Moja Oh, Simba, and I thought it was just the rain-god.

The thunder and rain continue. Moja and Stump Tooth take to their heels, seeking shelter. Moja stumbles over the body of the Lioness

(*Shouting over the storm*) Great Simba, what is this?

Stump Tooth It's your female! Run, Moja, run! The Devil-lion's after your blood.

They reach the cave

Moja (*seeing the cubs*) And what are these?

Stump Tooth They're your latest litter. Oh, Simba, (*falling to his knees*) I've been a bad lion, I've stolen the prey of my friends, spent too much time lying in the sun and generally wasted my days on earth. Spare us the wrath of the Devil-lion and I swear I'll become a reformed character.

Moja Be quiet! How can I think with you making all that noise? We don't know if it is the Devil-lion yet.

Stump Tooth It is, it is! Who else would kill your entire brood like that. Look at the shadows cast by his waving mane, and the flashes of light from his paws.

Moja Perhaps you're right. Mother of Simba and all the saint lions, what am I do do?

Stump Tooth (*praying*) Panthera leo, who are in heaven ...

Moja (*shouting*) I say, you up there, if you are the Devil-lion, listen to me!

The sound of the storm cuts out

Voice (*on amplifier*) What do you want?

Stump Tooth He spoke! Oh, Simba, though I walk through the valley of predatory-death, I shall fear no evil——

Moja I want to talk to you!

Voice What about?

Moja Are you really the Devil-lion or just some imposter?

An enormous roll of laughter which is echoed in rumbles of thunder

Voice My name is Thunder!

Moja That seems a funny name for a lion.

Voice My flying mane makes the whole world go dark. See, see how dark it is, and yet the sun has already scaled the sky for half-a-day. My giant paws flatten the ground and all the grazing fields for miles. As for my voice——

Moja Yes, yes, we know all about that. Let me see your face!

Voice —it deafens all who hear it.

Moja Well, there are some who say empty vessels make the most noise. Let me see your face and then I'll know whether to be afraid or not. (*Aside*) I'm only a small lion but he's not going to take my kingdom just by making a lot of noise. (*Calling*) Hey, you up there!

Voice How dare you!

Moja You know what the saying is. If a baby crawls under a bed and sits there, it'll grow up to be a dwarf. How do I know that's not what you are?

Voice What? Are you calling me a dwarf?

Stump Tooth (*all is lost*) Oh, Moja, what a fool you are . . .

Moja Yes! Unless you let me see your face.

Thunder. The face of the devil is seen—projection on to gauze or smoke

Voice There! look on my face and tremble.

Stump Tooth lets out a groan and buries his face. Even Moja is shaken

Moja Oh, Simba, show me what to do. Even I cannot hope to stand up to a demon like that.

1st Assistant And then he thought . . .

Moja What is this? I know this Thunder. In spite of his menacing mane and deep voice, I know he is only made of droplets of water.

1st Assistant And then he remembered something else.

Moja Stamp, Stump Tooth, stamp as if your life depended on it. (*He jumps to his feet and starts stamping loudly*)

Stump Tooth What is this, Moja? Have you gone *bata*?

1st Assistant Bats.

Moja Of course, I haven't I'm trying to shake the devil from the sky.

1st Assistant Moja had remembered something that the Ancients had said. Even the smallest movement can cause small winds that grow and grow and alter the whole behaviour of the sky. Of course it can take years and years.

Moja Stamp, Stump Tooth. Stamp everybody!

Stump Tooth begins to stamp. Soon everybody is stamping, spectators, even the Lioness and the cubs

Voice (*alarmed*) What is this? What are you up to down there?

Moja We're trying to shake you down like a rotten apple out of the sky. Come down here and face us, lion to lion!
All (*separately*) Yes, yes, come down here ... *etc.*

More stamping. Wind and thunder return to a crescendo, and then break off

Moja It's worked, it's worked.

A pause. The Devil-lion leaps into the clearing, wearing a demon mask and carrying an elaborate spear

Stump Tooth (*a shriek*) Oh, Simba, save us! (*He hides his face again*)
All (*separately*) Now's your chance, Moja. Kill him ... *etc.*
Moja (*aside*) Panthera leo, he's even worse than I thought. (*Aloud*) Jambo, Devil-king. Are you the one who wishes to take my kingdom from me?
Voice (*still on amplifier, but accompanied by mimed gestures by the masked demon*) Beware, Moja. You have defied my wrath and even shaken me like an apple from the sky. You cannot hope for mercy. Now I shall kill you.

The drums start. The stylized fight commences. Moja is unarmed, the Devil-lion uses his spear. The dancers cheer on Moja. Stump Tooth risks a glance or two and then with a cry goes back to his praying. After a great deal of leaping, shouting, spinning and grappling, Moja succeeds in grasping the spear and breaking it. Then he holds both points to the Devil's throat

Moja See what I've done. Now, Devil-lion, your days are numbered.
Voice Spare me, Moja. Let me go back to my sweet sky and I swear I'll never visit your country again.
Moja Very well, be gone. Remember it was I, Moja, Number One, King of the lions of Serengeti who has driven you from this place, and never show your mane or claws here again.

The Devil scurries off

Everybody cheers. Moja takes his bow very grandly. The sun comes out

Stump Tooth The sun, the sun! Oh, Moja, I promise I'll never, never doubt your courage again.
Moja (*grandly*) Yes, I was rather good, wasn't I? (*Aside*) Thank Simba he doesn't know I was like a jelly inside
1st Assistant So Moja drove the demon Thunder from his land and ruled unchallenged for the rest of his days. Unfortunately this meant that the Serengeti hardly gets any rain these days and an awful lot of animals die of thirst, but can you have a lot of good without at least a pinch of evil?
Moja I am Moja. My roaring fills the plains and raises the dust where the crops used to grow. Know what it says when you hear the sound ...

Amplified sound effect of lions' roaring

Who is the King of the Jungle? I am ... I am ... I am!

Applause

The Lion's party remove their masks, take their bows and run off

The Dancers talk excitedly, Tangaroa and the Wise Ones confer. The Recorder chips away in a flurry

Recorder (*to his neighbour*) What came after, "Can you have a lot of good"?

Neighbour (*showing him*) "Without at least a *pinch* of evil."

Storyteller (*after congratulating his Assistant, to everybody who will listen*) What a very *scientific* lion. And it's true, you know? Weather is made up by many things—water, wind, clouds, land, the heat of the sun, even the sea. Quite small things, even a man running, can stir and air and make the most *enormous* changes if only you wait long enough.

1st Wise One But do we want science from a lion? I prefer my knowledge to come from books.

2nd Wise One And he wasn't very brave and he didn't hunt. Surely one expects a lion to hunt . . .

3rd Wise One I thought he was brave. Do they not tell us that real courage—absolute courage, that is—can only be shown when the knowledge of fear is present?

4th Wise One That's all too complicated for me. In fact the whole thing was too complicated. Why don't they have stories like they used to have, with a proper beginning, middle and an end?

Storyteller Shall the lion be condemned then simply because he did not conform to your picture of him? Did he not act the best way he could to defend his territory? And do we not do that every day?

The Dancers agree or disagree as the spirit takes them

Chamberlain (*bowing with huge ritual to the god*) Great Tangaroa, is it your wish that we should vote on the lion's case now?

Tangaroa D-d-d-d . . . b-b-b-b . . . m-m-m-m . . .

Chamberlain (*bowing low and addressing the Court*) The god commands that all twelve candidates be seen first and the scores announced at the end.

Excited (*to her neighbour*) Just like the Miss World Contest.

Talkative Who's next? I can't wait to hear the result. I quite liked the lion, but I thought his mate was too strict with the cubs. But he'd have my vote, although do you remember the woodpecker from the last round. I thought he deserved to be one of the finalists . . .

Adenoidal I preferred the snout-beetle.

Affected The Hairedale for me.

Motherly Oh, I liked the rabbits.

Logical You couldn't choose the rabbits.

Motherly Why not?

Logical Just imagine a world populated by five species and the rabbits. The others wouldn't get a look in.

All What comes next? What comes next?

The Chamberlain has been conferring with the Court. Now he advances, clears his throat, bangs with his staff and announces

Chamberlain Lophornis magnifica!

The clerks repeat the cry as before

All What's that?

Chamberlain The humming bird!

All (*separately*) The humming-bird? Oh, how beautiful, what a surprise . . . etc.

The Lights reveal the Elephant bowing and nodding

Huge laughter from the Spectators

Chamberlain (*outraged*) What's this? What's this? You're not a humming-bird!

Rajah I'm Rajah, the More or Less Elephant who wanted to get on in the world.

Chamberlain Well, go away, go away! Your name is way down the list. I'm not at all sure the Court will want to see you now.

Vedda, the little mahout, comes running on

Vedda (*to Rajah*) Where have you been? I've been looking everywhere for you. You've been very, very naughty . . . very naughty indeed. (*Leading him away*)

Rajah (*sadly*) I only wanted my chance to survive . . .

Vedda But not now, not now.

They go out accompanied by great laughter and ironic applause

Chamberlain (*glaring after them*) The humming-bird!

The Lights change. The drums start a slow rhythm. The Dancers hum a song without words

The Humming-bird runs on, bows and settles

The 2nd Assistant Storyteller steps forward

2nd Assistant There are many, many kinds of humming-birds. This one in the plumage of the male Lophornis magnifica represents all. Some humming-birds are so small that they weigh only one-fifteenth of an ounce! But so strong that, even at that size, their wings beat about eighty times *a second*! This makes them the only birds in the whole world that can fly backwards, sideways or even hover immobile in mid-air. It is on this miracle of nature that the humming-bird rests its case.

The Assistant steps back, the music continues. The Humming-bird speaks

Humming-bird Two hundred years ago, the wise ones of the world gathered together to discuss the beauty of my wings. "Such colours do not exist," they cried. "Such greens, such reds, such midnight blues! See, if you view them one way, they are one shade. But seen from another, they become infinitely different." Then they invented a glass, a magic thing with which they could inspect the secrets of my plumage. "See," they cried, "the colours do *not* exist. Close to, there is nothing there." Then one two-legged wiser than the rest—they addressed him thus, "Sir Isaac of the

New-town", spied the answer. "Behold," he said, "the trick lies not in the plumage itself but in the filmy plate of moisture that covers the tips. This so reflects, refracts the light, that colour appears where once there was none. Truly this is a miracle of nature." Thus spake Sir Newton and was honoured above kings for his discovery. (*She preens, spreads her wings, settles in another area*) As for my strength, eighty beats a second is really nothing to me. To hang motionless in the air requires one hundred and twenty beats a second! So fast the movement, so strong the pull of my muscles, it cannot be seen with the naked eye. To equal my strength to size, a swan ... such a very over-praised bird, I always think ... would have to have a wingspan sixty-five feet across.

And I hover
And dart,
And roll in the air.

Back
And forth
And here
And there,
I speed,
Arrow-like,
A very little
Bird,
A flash of
Fire,
Pure movement.

Gone before
You see,
Or staying
Motionless
Long after
You have gone.

Down to the
Nectar
In the
Forests of
Brazil,
Touching—
And yet not
Touching—
My long
Beak and
The split-tongue
It conceals
Resting not
In

But barely
On
The flamevine
Blossom,
The transparent
Tongue
Draws up the
Sugar liquid,
The nectar
Which I need
Drop by drop.

And all
The time,
My wings,
My mighty chest,
Less than
One-fifteenth
Of an ounce
In size,
Beats,
Beats
A hundred times
A second
To keep me hanging
There.

And then
With one
Swift roll,
I pivot
Back so
Sharply
That my
Shoulders twist
Half-round —
Yes, one hundred
And eighty
Degrees to
Provide the
Lift for
Movement. Then
Godlike I
Rise vertically in the
Air, or —
Tilting back
And beating
At the wind
I dart forward

Or back
Using rearward
Thrust. In
Less than
Two-tenths
Of a second,
Beating all
The time,
I have
Backed,
Banked,
Rolled and
Thrust
And in the
Time it takes
For you to
Blink an eye,
I have sucked
Another blossom
Dry.
Thus modestly,
But knowing I
Can count on
You,
I say
No universe
Deserves to be,
If it does
Not consider
Me.

She rises, beats and goes

2nd Assistant That is her song. Let it go from her to you.

Applause. The drums change rhythm. Everybody moves to new positions

1st Wise One Well, she was pretty. I'll give her that.
2nd Wise One But what good is she?
3rd Wise One (*worried*) Does she have to do good to survive?
1st Wise One Of course! Naturally.
3rd Wise One Can't she just be herself? Beautiful?
1st Wise One Nonsense!
2nd Wise One Rubbish!
3rd Wise One (*still worried*) It could be that in simply being beautiful she is singing her hymn of praise to her creator.
Storyteller (*coming forward*) Two down and ten to go. The tension rises. Think, think of what this means. Of all the beauties of the universe—the insects, plants, birds and fishes—from potter wasp and squid and octopus, from albatross and flying bat, from cottonwood spore, rattler

and sidewinder, to water-spider, lynx and daddy longlegs, frog, otter, weaver-bird and the plum-tree at the bottom of your garden—all but six must go. Oh, Tuan god, I hope you know what you are doing. So much beauty, so much wonder, swept away! Who will feed the ox when the grass is gone? How will the grass grow when the worms have died? How can the worms survive if the tiniest grubs they live on have perished? Watch the oak topple if the land it stands on is dead. See the fishes floating belly up, the birds fall from the sky, for each is dependent one on the other, just as you and I and all of us, hang on each other to stay alive. Think of all this and see the mighty task, the grave task which rests on our little god's shoulders.

Chamberlain What a lot of fuss about nothing. Trust in the god. He'll know what to do.

Storyteller So speak the lordly ones by parliamentary bill or government white paper, tearing forests down, damming rivers up, changing hills from here to there, digging holes where nature has provided none and all . . . or so much . . . without *thought*, and coming back later and saying, "If only we'd known", or, "If only you'd told us", or, even "It wasn't us but the other Party that is to blame", and letting the earth die or dry up and go rotten so that the fish reek before they have died because of the mercury in the rivers or the filth in the sea, and birds shrivel on the branch because of chemicals in the air, and gulls struggle helplessly on the shore because an oil-tanker's captain lost control ten miles from collision-point and piled his vessel on a rock. So speak the lordly ones—"We'll give you ten thousand as compensation", but the seagull dies and one more miracle of nature goes out. So much fuss about nothing? Oh, well, perhaps he's right. Take everything seriously but yourself, they do say. Here I am forgetting that very thing.

Chamberlain Case the Third!

Cheeky Boy The elephant?

Chamberlain (*frowning angrily*) The whale!

Clerks The whale . . . the whale . . . the whale . . .!

A crash on the gong. All the Dancers and anybody else who can be spared race to the centre and form the whale's body that pulsates and trembles and threshes with its tail. The headpiece is carried on

3rd Assistant He is Orca. The lion speaks for courage, the humming-bird for skill. He speaks for size.

The sound of heavy waves breaking and sea-birds and then a series of shrill piping notes like those sent out by Asdic sounders which take us down . . . down into the ocean. The Lights go green, projections ripple, all movement stills

Deep down at the foot of the world, far from the sight of man, in the land of the Long Dark and Consistent Ice in the region of the (*carefully*) Ant-art-ic-a, there lived a pack of killer whales of which Orca was the biggest and strongest. But amongst themselves whales don't savage or maim and Orca's days were spent sporting in freezing sea and searching for food to keep his huge body warm. Do you know how whales feed? Sometimes they simply open their mouths and let the food flow in. Others dive at the bottom and scoop up everything they find. Filters do the rest. What a miracle of god is Whale—a whole floating factory, a sub-continent, all by itself.

An amplified groan from Orca

Orca Deep down in the belly of the sea where the water is green and the sun never reaches, the happy whales sport and roll.

The song of the whales is heard—moans and cries, heartbreaking in the echoes of loneliness they evoke

See the white world tremble as we heave into sight, dancing on our tails a hundred foot above the ocean. Poised there, big as clouds, wriggling our jelly-fat with delight, we greet the sun. Then back into the water—what a joyous crash, what a slithering and sliding of exploding water, of fresh bright crystals and mindshaking sideslip of ocean. "Oh, great god Balaena," we cry—for we are very religious creatures, "Oh great god Balaena, how we adore you. God of the little whales, be pleased with us."

The actors forming the whale's body squirm and thrash with joy while Orca cries out his happiness

Whale-heaven must be a place very like this, we often think only without the troubles, so we spend our days trying to make a tiny heaven out of our piece of sea.

Sailors (*off; the traditional cry*) There she blows!
Orca From snout to tail—sixty foot in length—I quiver all over at the thought of Balaena hearing our call. Was ever a god so loved!
Sailors (*off*) There she blows!

They move into sight keeping in formation as if rowing, but making a team dance of menace as they approach Orca

Orca There's nothing we whales would rather do than contemplate in tranquility the beauty of the whale-universe.

The music takes up the theme of the hunt. The Sailors approach warily—still keeping in time and formation—while Orca, all unknowing, swims and thrashes contentedly. Then, on cue, the invisible harpoons are launched! Uproar! Orca rears up and bellows with surprise. Great movement by the "body", the Sailors find their boat swamped and are pitched overboard. Orca keeps up a roaring of rage and shock

What's this, what's this? An attack has been made on me! What have I done? Great Balaena, see this outrage and tell me what to do.

During the uproar, one of the Sailors grabs hold of the raft—the base of the palanquin used for Tangaroa—and scrambles aboard. Instantly the other Sailors lift him high and swoop him around the acting area, simulating the movements of the churning sea

Sailor (*terrified*) Heaven help me! Now I must surely die! Where are my
dear companions? God save me. I am alone on this raft of mine and below
me there are nothing but the icy depths.

Orca (*bellowing at the same time*) Balaena, save your little whale! What
must I do? I know nothing of violence. I fear for my life!

The raft is carried close to Orca's head

Great god of us all, what is it? It has a flat base and tiny head ... a
monster, a monster!

Sailor (*seeing Orca*) The whale, the whale! Heaven save me from his jaws.

The raft is carried away again. The uproar slowly dies

Orca What a raucous screeching. It quite hurt my ears. Can it really be a
monster? There it is again. (*Calling*) What are you, you strange finless
creature? Can you really be a fish?

Sailor (*still hanging on to the raft for dear life*) What do you think I am, you
stupid whale? I'm a man, of course.

Orca What manner of beast is that? An aman! Does it swim or fly or crawl
like a crab?

Sailor I WALK, of course! That is ... when I get the chance.

Orca Walk? How fascinating. But I can see no legs. Will you show me?

Sailor How can I? Not on this stupid raft.

Orca I know! I know! Walk on me.

3rd Assistant Then by keeping very still Orca allowed the raft to come
alongside.

*The boys bring the raft to Orca and the Sailor scrambles on to his back in a
very undignified fashion. He clings to it too terrified to move*

Orca (*intrigued*) Well, now, will you show me how you walk?

Sailor Not at the moment, thank you very much. Your back is too slippery
with oil and water, I'd never keep my footing.

Orca How very limited you amans are. I can swim and dive and fly if I
choose to.

Sailor Fly? I don't believe you.

Orca Well, I can dance on my tail, which amounts to the same thing. Shall I
show you?

Sailor No-o-o, thank you!

Orca Pity, I'm the best dancer in the whole pack. Even the young calves
can't dance like Orca does. What are you doing here anyway, if you can't
swim like a fish, fly like a gull or crawl like a crab?

Sailor I came hunting you, of course.

Orca Hunting, what is that?

Sailor Well, to put it another way ... I came to make your acquaintance.

Orca That's very civil of you, very civil indeed. My name is Orca.

Sailor And mine is Matthew.

Orca Well, now that we've met is there any place you'd like to visit?

Sailor I wouldn't mind going somewhere warmer if it's all the same to you.

Orca No sooner said than done. Hang on.

3rd Assistant So off they set, swimming strongly, from the land of the Ant-art-ic-a, up the coast of Africa until they came to the place of the warmer sea where the Matthew aman began to thaw out. And all the time they travelled they discussed many things—philosophy, poetry, the science of things—what makes water boil and things like that—the ballet, and the behaviour of the stars in the sky. By the time they came to the tropics, Orca was thinking . . .

Orca This aman is really very interesting. In spite of his limited ways I can learn a lot from him.

3rd Assistant While the sailor was thinking . . .

Sailor What a very obliging fellow this whale is. I'm sure if I asked him he'd take me all the way back to Southampton.

3rd Assistant And at that very moment there came into view the self-same ship Matthew had sailed on two years before. And the sailors, catching sight of the comrade they'd given up for lost, set up a great hurraying and hulloing.

Cries of, "Welcome back, Matthew", and "Who's your friend?" etc.

Orca What very friendly creatures. Are they acquaintances of yours also?

Sailor Yes, they're the people I came hunting you with . . .

3rd Assistant And then, remembering why he'd gone to the Ant-art-ic-a in the first place and overcome with the thought of all that whale-oil, wax and bone meal, ambergris, guano and liver that he was sitting on, he drew his little knife and stabbed Orca in the eye.

The Sailor hangs on as Orca sends up a loud cry of pain and thrashes about bewildered

Orca What's this? I've brought you all the way from the beautiful waters of the whale-world to the turgid place of the aman-people and you've rewarded me with death!

Sailor I'm sorry, Orca. (*He keeps on stabbing*) That's the way it is.

3rd Assistant And in no time at all the water was flowing red and Orca found himself swimming with Balaena in whale-heaven, which is a place very like the Ant-art-ic-a—only without the troubles.

Orca At least you know who your friends are.

3rd Assistant As for the sailor . . .

Sailor I am Matthew the Sailor and I'll tell you this. I've made enough money from this one stupid whale to buy a whole fleet of ships of my own!

Cheers from his friends

1st Wise One Bah! What a very silly story. It just goes to show how expendable whales are!

2nd Wise One I thought he was going to tell us about strength. It seems to me he only showed us how easily he was defeated.

3rd Wise One (*worried*) I don't know. What about trust? Isn't there a place in our universe for something like that?

4th Wise One Well, I couldn't make head or tail of it. There was no proper narrative line, if you follow me.

Chamberlain Shh-h! It's not over yet.

Orca Deep down in the fathomless depths, the whales rock with delight, seeing with tiny eyes an horizon twice the length of time, where giant beasts roamed the sky long before the earth was made. (*Bellowing*) Oh, Balaena, Balaena, we worship you!

1st Wise One There you are! Just an anachronism!

Storyteller But shouldn't we have some of those? A world without anachronisms is a world without history.

2nd Wise One History is junk! Who wants it?

Storyteller You may not want it, but you've got it. Anything that lives longer than a millionth of a millionth of a millionth of a second has a past ... and what is that but history?

3rd Wise One (*still worried*) Yes, I can see that, but perhaps the great god Tuan deserves to have only modern things in this new universe of his.

Storyteller Oh, my friend, in all the wonders of the world, what is "modern"? What is even "new"?

1st Wise One I still say this is a very poor selection of stories.

2nd Wise One Here, here. The lion boasts of courage and only tells us how cowardly he is. The humming-bird boasts of skill and beauty, but admits that even the beauty is a trick. And the whale talks of size and is proved to be no larger than a pen-knife!

4th Wise One And I couldn't understand any of them.

Uproar. Some argue this way, others that. The Storyteller silences them with a gesture

Storyteller Perhaps the moral is that nobody knows where his strongest points lie.

The Lights slowly return to normal as the argument continues. Orca speaks bewildered

Orca Does that mean they didn't like my story?

The "body" breaks up. As they go back to their places one of the Dancers pats the whale on the head

Dancer Never mind, Orca, we loved you.

Orca (*a cry of sadness*) But even we whales have a right to survive.

All the members of the cast choose a name of a species and the cry is taken up: "So have the jackals ... the elm trees ... the bluebottles" etc. Off stage, as if disturbed by this clamour, there starts a giant trumpetting, roaring, chirping and twittering. The Chamberlain waves demented arms

Chamberlain (*shouting to the Dancers*) Now see what you've done! (*To the species off-stage*) BE QUIET! Unless we have law and order NOBODY will be selected.

The panic slowly subsides

Storyteller (*shaking his head*) It was bound to happen. When you have a hundred thousand to choose from, it's easy to say no. No to the nettles because they scratch you, no to the snakes because they bite you, no to the spiders and mosquitoes because they sting you . . . so easy in fact that now it is very difficult to find a reason for saying yes. Yes to the lion because he behaved nobly, yes to the humming-bird because she is beautiful, yes to the whale because she behaved gallantly. Oh, Tuan, great god, you have asked us to test the species. Sometimes I think you are testing us more.

Chamberlain Silence for Case the Fourth. (*Aside to the Storyteller*) Anarchist! (*He looks at his scroll*) What is this? No, it cannot be!

Cheeky Boy The elephant?

All Shh-h!

An expectant pause. The Chamberlain tries to announce the name

Chamberlain The . . . (*and gives up in shame*)

The loud braying of a Donkey is heard. Everybody falls about with laughter

The Donkey wanders on and watches them sadly. As the laughter starts to die, he says patiently

Donkey I can wait.

Which starts them off again. The Chamberlain does his best to restore the dignity of the Court

Chamberlain Be quiet, be quiet, how dare you. (*To the Donkey*) Really I do apologize, but, well, honestly . . .

The laughter finally dies. Somebody runs forward and puts a rope halter around the Donkey's neck. Another ties a blindfold over her eyes

Donkey I walk. (*She sets off. Tethered by the halter, she simply plods round and round in a circle while she speaks*) I never know when the sun comes up or when it sets. I have never known the feel of any other stones but these which I have trodden since I was a foal. Round and round I go, turning the wheel which draws water from the well to wet the ground from which the meagre strands of millet grow. I know the sun shines for it burns the scars on my neck where the rope rubs, and I know when the wind blows because it fills my ears with dust. Can you wonder there are times when I won't budge? I stick my forelegs into the ground and refuse to give an inch. Oh, then they go mad. They prod me with sticks and flog me with whips and pull on my ears and put their shoulders to my flanks, but do you think we haven't got our dignity also? What sort of life is this? Are we not allowed our share of fulfilment also? Others of my kind, here in this land of brittle rock and sun and sand, are loaded up with packs as big as houses—of corn, straw, wood and stones—you would say, "There is a cottage moving on four little legs"—and for good measure a man or half-a-dozen children as well, and off they go, trotting, trotting . . . but we have our secret understandings. We *know* when we see one another, we know we are the chosen. You despise us for not being as big as horses, or as small as dogs, but we know we had our moment of glory when a king rode on our back and palm-leaves fell about our feet. We know. You call us

"stupid" and each other, "stupid as donkeys", but we think of ourselves
as patient. We know our time will come again . . . will come . . . will come
. . . will come . . . will come . . . will come . . . will come . . . will come. . . will
come . . . will come . . .

She is led from the stage

A long ashamed silence. The 3rd Wise One says to the 4th

3rd Wise One (*ironically*) Did you understand *that*?

*The discussion is interrupted by the appearance of a Messenger, frightened
and out of breath. He flings himself on his knees in front of the god and
grovels unhappily*

Messenger Oh, mighty Tanga. Lord of the sky and earth, forgive me——
Chamberlain Who is this? What are you that addresses the god?
Messenger —forgive this poor man the terrible news he brings.
All (*separately*) What news? Who is this man? What's happened? . . . *etc.*
Messenger (*to Tanga*) It's not my fault, I swear on my ancestors. I was
simply sent with the message.
Chamberlain What message? Who are you? How dare you interrupt the
proceedings of the Court?
Messenger (*grovelling to the Chamberlain*) Oh, mighty holyship, forgive this
fool his presumption. I come to tell you of another candidate.
Chamberlain Another candidate? Impossible!
All (*separately*) Yes, yes, impossible . . . *etc.*
Chamberlain The law allows for only twelve today. The final twelve from
whom we must pick six to survive.
All (*separately*) Yes, that's right, only twelve . . . *etc.*
Chamberlain (*to the Messenger*) So tell this impudent . . . thing to be gone!
Messenger But, my lord, I cannot! It is . . . a human being!

Shocked reaction from everybody

Chamberlain But that . . . that is ridiculous.
1st Wise One Impossible!
2nd Wise One Nonsense!
3rd Wise One Surely it was taken for granted——
4th Wise One That *we* should survive?
3rd Wise One Wasn't it?
Recorder (*still chipping away like mad*) What did he say it was?
Neighbour (*still shocked*) A human being!
1st Wise One (*to the Chamberlain*) Well, wasn't it?
Chamberlain Taken for granted? Yes, yes, of course . . . well, I assume it was
. . . (*To Tanga*) Great god . . . ?

*A reaction from everybody. The Human has come on. Like most of the parts
it can be played by a boy or a girl, but here it is written for a girl*

Who are you? Why have you come?
Human To stand my trial with the others.
Chamberlain But who sent you? Who is responsible for this . . . joke?

Human The great god Tuan.

Another shocked reaction

Chamberlain But I cannot conceive . . . (*to Tanga*) My lord, can it be that Tuan himself is preparing to destroy mankind?
Tangaroa (*helplessly*) B-b-b-b . . . d-d-d-d . . . m-m-m-m . . .
Chamberlain (*turning away sadly*) He does not know.
1st Wise One Well, I say it's nonsense!
2nd Wise One So do I!
4th Wise One It's obvious Tuan intended to save us!
3rd Wise One (*worried*) Is it?
1st Wise One Of course it is! Aren't we his favourite species?
All Yes, yes, yes!
1st Wise One So I say, ignore the message!
2nd Wise One Or else . . . there is another way. (*He exchanges a look with the 1st Wise One*)
All (*separately*) What does he mean? Another way? . . . etc.
2nd Wise One It's simple. Throw out one of the others. We have to choose six, don't we? Very well. Choose five. Mankind itself will be the sixth.
All (*separately*) Of course! What a very simple solution . . . etc.

General rejoicing

Storyteller What a very simple solution . . . or so they thought. But then a very strange thing occurred. From the ranks of all the other species awaiting the verdict . . . a murmur . . . a shouting . . . a positive hurricane of protest arose.

General uproar off stage. The Lion, the Humming-bird, the Whale and the Donkey reappear. Even the Elephant hovers unhappily in the wings.

Moja (*to Tanga*) My lord, we must protest!
Chamberlain Protest?
Humming-bird All the species say this cannot be.
All (*separately*) How dare they? They're only birds, animals . . . etc.
Orca Who is man to have this favoured treatment?
Rajah (*trumpetting*) Yes, who, who?
Orca A man killed me.
Moja He kills me every day.
Donkey He makes my life a living burden.
Chamberlain How dare you? Go away, go away!
Humming-bird Why should he be spared his trial when even Tuan doesn't think so?
Rajah Yes, why, why?
Chamberlain (*pompously*) I'll tell you why—because he is the Lord of the Universe!

Huge laughter from the animals, echoed and re-echoed off-stage

Storyteller So now, impasse had arrived.
Moja We'll tell you this. If you choose mankind without making him stand trial with the rest of us, we . . . we would prefer to die.

Chamberlain (*aghast*) What? You'd go on strike?

Moja (*nodding*) Everything would die. The fish, the birds, the animals. Even the crops in the fields. Where would your man be then? That is our last word.

The Animals leave

A shocked pause

Storyteller So for the first time they learnt of the hatred with which the other living things viewed them.

Chamberlain But this is terrible . . . terrible . . . what shall we do?

All (*separately*) Terrible, terrible. Of course you could let man stand his trial . . . but if we should lose? . . . *etc.*

Chamberlain The Court is adjourned. The god must have time to think this over. Go away, go away, all of you!

Clerks (*clearing the Court*) Adjourned . . . adjourned!

The drums start. The Lights start to fade leaving the Storyteller in a single spotlight. Everybody else is hidden in the dark

Storyteller Terrible, indeed! What will be the outcome, what will they do? (*Looking up with a gentle smile*) I tell you, Tuan, you have set them quite a problem. (*He bows as before, turns to go and then turns back again*) Set *us* quite a problem. What can we do? (*He looks up at the spotlight and gives a gentle puff*)

The spotlight goes out. The drums stop

ACT II

Before the interval ends, the Court and Dancers reappear and take their positions in silence. This time the latter bring with them placards of their own making, strips of card on short poles, each bearing the names of the six species they'd most like to save. These are put to one side, face down, before the action starts. For the last minute the Drummers build up a fast rhythm which leads up to the entrance of the Storyteller. He makes sure all is ready, nods to the Drummers, bows to the audience, the drums break off and the Lights go down

A single spotlight picks out Aquila the Golden Eagle in as high a place as possible

Aquila I am Aquila! I am Eagle! (*She stretches her wings. They should span seven feet at least*)

An impressed reaction from the spectators, as the Lights increase

(*With hatred*) Know from the beginning my implacable contempt for man. Like my fellows I protest at this fascist-imperialist behaviour of a sub-species which enables it to grab half the world as his and set itself up as our judge. By what right does he do this?
Chamberlain (*indignantly*) This is out of order. How dare you question the Court?
Aquila Does the god judge us?
Chamberlain ... Yes.
Aquila Then what are they, your so-called Wise Ones?
Chamberlain They ... advise.
Aquila You lie! The god is silent. (*Drawing herself up*) I shall not be judged by such as they.

A shocked silence

1st Wise One This ... is intolerable.
2nd Wise One I don't see why.
4th Wise One If we don't judge, who will?
3rd Wise One What is it saying, what is it saying?
1st Wise One There is nothing better to judge these things than mankind. This is a man-Court.
Recorder (*to Neighbour*) Do I have to write all this down?
Aquila What did you say, so-called Wise One?
1st Wise One I said, who is better qualified to judge than we?
Aquila You set yourself above the god?
1st Wise One No, I only meant——

Aquila Let Tangaroa speak!

Reaction from the spectators. Some: "She is right", others: "Shocking! Who is she to demand", etc.

Chamberlain He cannot speak except through me.

Aquila So now you claim to be the god's brain and mouth. Are you perhaps the god?

Chamberlain (*defiant*) In many ways, yes!

A reaction of horror. The gong strikes. Tangaroa stands. All fall flat on their faces, the Chamberlain as well

Tangaroa (*it starts as a series of sounds*) . . . amply inquire vandals now it is broken and paintwork scratched for we have no site but a rubbish dump in asking a great deal for the search after he was kidnapped and terrorists pulled off his wings and front doors and windows made of stainless steel and nuclear fission in a police court appearance on divan sets going cheap with headboards extra and long and straight as an arrow flying in Concorde when it was announced that sex and the prostate gland did more to cause poverty in these days of social welfare and reliable television service from house to house where the nurse's ordeal with the burglar did more to offset rate debates for the kiss of life to the green pound and ten per cent this year and perhaps an Electrolux next. (*He sits and composes himself as before*)

Chamberlain (*after a moment, awed*) The god has spoken.

All (*separately, scrambling to their feet*) Yes, he has spoken . . . *etc.*

Aquila But what did he say?

Chamberlain That you must be judged by us.

Aquila Liar. Liar. Liar.

The screaming of eagles fills the theatre

Hear me, O my brothers. You who crawl on the earth, dig beneath its surface, swim its seas, brush the sky with your branches or skim the face of the great god himself with your wings — you, you alone, shall be my judges. My peers, nothing but my peers, that's what I demand.

Moja, Orca the Humming-bird and Donkey enter and take their places opposite the Wise Ones

Moja Now we are here.

Chamberlain (*in an apoplexy*) What is this? You can't take over the Court!

Donkey Try and get rid of us.

Orca Speak, Aquila.

Aquila Then, listen.

The Lights change until only the spotlight remains on the Eagle. A single melodic line emerges like that of a reed-pipe

In the rough foothill country of Southern Montana in a piece of ranchland more than a third of the size of the Yellowstone Park, I reign supreme. Hemmed in by the Bridger Mountains, the Crazy and Absar-

oka, I soar the buttes and ridges, eleven thousand feet above sea-level.
For I am the King of the Birds. Once—once my image led the Roman
legions into battle. Persian hordes followed me in their conquest. Indians
wore my flight feathers in their war-bonnets. In the time of Kublai Khan,
the great Marco Polo wrote "In China they even have eagles trained to
kill wolves, foxes, deer and wild goats." As a boy Genghis Khan called
himself Temujin which means Rider of Heaven. I am Temujin, I am
Aquila, I am Eagle. My friendship has been claimed by the greatest
warriors. Alexander rode with me on his wrist to face Darius at Arbela.
Agamemnon flew me before he captured Troy. Anthony chose me as his
confidant before Philippi. I rode the Lionheart's shoulder at the Siege of
Acre. I am Eagle. My screaming fills your ears when I plunge from my
perch to the quivering earth. You have even copied this by attaching such
screams to your flying machines when they drop to scatter haphazard
death. But there is nothing haphazard in the death I bring. From so high
you with your puny eyes would not see, I sight a mole, a jackrabbit
squatting among the protective rocks. Dropping, with shields closing
automatically over my eyes against the racing winds, my wings folded
aerodynamically to increase the speed, I pinpoint the huddled prey and
swoop so close—with iron talons extended—talons so strong they'd pin
your hand to the wood—that the quivering creature feels my breath, and
yet so powerfully that by extending my enormous wings and thrusting
with my chest, I am mounting the sky again before his fellows have had a
chance to move.

The Lights come up again

Chamberlain This is too much. You are a scavenger!
Aquila I kill to live. CAN YOU SAY THE SAME?
1st Wise One Sheep, chickens——
Aquila The impedimenta of a feeble sub-species. Are my young not entitled
to food?
2nd Wise One We hunt you!
Aquila Yes, you have hunted me. Your scouts have climbed the rocks and
invaded the eyries. You have broken the nests, stoned the eaglets, shot,
poisoned, trapped and destroyed thousands at a time. In some places you
have even called it sport to follow us in your flying machines and shoot at
us on the wing. Less of our number exist every year. If you had your way,
we should all die tomorrow.
1st Wise One I tell you, you are a public menace. Every year you carry off
lambs——
Aquila In my mountainlands alone, eighteen thousand lambs are produced
each year. Last year only two lambs were found in our nests and they were
carrion. Why should I kill a lamb when with these talons I can destroy a
full-grown mule deer, a pronghorn antelope, caribou or reindeer?
2nd Wise One But we shall kill you!
Aquila Yes, you'll kill us. The poisons you are putting in the earth are
destroying us, nest by nest, or driving us mad or causing malformations in
a species so proud that the Indians of my country called us brothers.

The drums start a halting beat

And where are they now, the brothers Shawnee, Chicasaw, Choctaw, Sioux, Chippewa, Apache, Shoshone and Wichita? And where shall we be tomorrow? For now you've taken *our* gods, *our* identity—you've taken everything!

The screaming of the eagles returns

(*Over the uproar*) Hear me, Black Elk ... Red Cloud ... Little Wolf ... Great White Eagle, how I curse the destroyers ... curse them! ... curse them! ... curse them!

The screaming and the Lights go down together. The Storyteller emerges into his spotlight

Storyteller Yes, well, our story has changed, I can see that. But you want to know about that other business, what we intend to do about the human candidate. Taking all things into consideration, we've decided he must present his case with the others. And how did we make space for him, you'll ask. Ah, such ingenuity. Three of the species who feel they can only live *with* man, offered to include him with their case. So he'll get his chance. Yes, they'll all get their chance. But first——

The Lights increase

4th Wise One I really must protest at the way politics have been brought into this. Fascist-imperialists he called us.
3rd Wise One Well, we have rather grabbed everything for ourselves.
4th Wise One For their own good!
3rd Wise One They don't seem to think so. Anyway, when was the last time you heard of an animal using a man for vivisection?
1st Wise One I for one won't accept the eagle. He's bigoted and bitter!
Storyteller Could it be yourself in him you fear?
1st Wise One Never! Lies! Lies!
Moja Come, my brothers, we shall now vote on Aquila.
Chamberlain What! You can't do that!
Humming-bird Why not? You heard what she said. She'd only be judged by her peers.
Chamberlain But ... you have no rights here!
Donkey Have you?
Orca As it is there are only four of us and five of you.
3rd Wise One I'll stand down.
Chamberlain But they are the Wise Ones!
Donkey Do they know what it's like to be a donkey ... a lion ... a humming-bird?
Aquila (*from her perch*) I shall make up the fifth. Proceed.
Moja Proceed.
Orca Proceed.
Cheeky Boy The elephant. Can we hear the elephant now?
Clerks The elephant ... the elephant ... the elephant.

Chamberlain (*in despair*) What will they do when it comes to man?
3rd Wise One Perhaps for once he'll have to stand on his two feet.

The Chamberlain glares at him. The Lights starts to go down. The 4th Assistant Storyteller steps forward

4th Assistant This is my story. Let it go from me to you. Close to the west coast of the Resplendent Land which is the home of the Lion People or Sinhalese, near the village of Ratnapura which is situated in some of the thickest jungle of those parts, lived a colony of langur monkeys who had decided they were human.

The music starts. The Dancers rise and scatter as monkeys. Some prowl, others climb, all chatter. In no time at all they have reached the most unlikely places in the theatre. Shafts of light pierce the thick foliage. Tropical noises— frogs, insects and the screeching of wild birds—are heard

Once a year they came together to review their progress.
1st Monkey I think we're doing very well.
2nd Monkey Not so well.
3rd Monkey Badly.
4th Monkey Oh, I don't know. It could be worse.
5th Monkey Much worse.
6th Monkey Absolutely awful. We could still be living in the trees.
7th Monkey Instead of houses.
8th Monkey With three bedrooms.
9th Monkey Indoor sanitation.
10th Monkey And a garage for each pair of families.
11th Monkey The trouble is——
12th Monkey You've said it!
13th Monkey There are no cars in the garages——
14th Monkey No gas-stoves in the kitchens——
15th Monkey No deep-freezers——
16th Monkey And not a washing machine in sight!
17th Monkey (*to the 1st*) So how can you sit there looking smug——
18th Monkey —beats me.
1st Monkey (*equably*) Oh, well it was a way of getting the discussion started. What do the rest of you think?
19th Monkey We want more money.
20th Monkey Cordon bleu cooking.
21st Monkey A disco——
22nd Monkey A strip-club.
23rd Monkey A zoo.
24th Monkey Money.
25th Monkey Money.
26th Monkey (*by now we're probably going round again*) Money.
27th Monkey (*or whatever*) Money.
28th Monkey Something to look up to.
1st Monkey Which means money also, I suppose.

28th Monkey Not necessarily. It could be a purpose in life. Something like that. (*Giving up*) I don't know.
1st Monkey I know exactly what you mean. Something to live for. That's what we want. It's time we monkeys moved into heavy industry.
All Industry?
1st Monkey Look around you. What do you see?
2nd Monkey Nothing but trees.
3rd Monkey Trees.
4th Monkey Trees.
5th Monkey And the occasional creeper.
1st Monkey So what's happening on the rest of the island? They're chopping down the trees and selling them. Right?
6th Monkey Right!
7th Monkey Are we going to do that?
1st Monkey Why not? It's big business.
8th Monkey But we'd need machinery. Heavy trucks and so on.
1st Monkey Very well. Scatter and find us a truck.

They rise from wherever they've been, race about and take up new positions

9th Monkey Nothing.
10th Monkey Nothing.
11th Monkey Not a Dodge in sight.
12th Monkey Hang on, there's something coming.

Rajah lumbers in with Vedda, the Mahout, on his shoulders

13th Monkey Just a crummy old elephant.
Rajah Hearing of your needs, I decided to offer myself. I'm Rajah, you see, the More or Less Elephant who wants to get on in the world.
14th Monkey What do you know! An elephant with pretentions!
Vedda It's no more pretentious than a lot of monkeys who think they're human. I'm Vedda his driver. (*Pretending to drive a car*) Vroooooooom— Vrooooooooo! I'm a good driver——
Rajah And I can do anything a bulldozer can. I can drag one thousand pound loads through the forest, need no spare parts, yearly tune-ups or imported fuel. What's more I give a guarantee. Fifty years.
2nd Monkey (*to the 1st*) What do you think?
1st Monkey OK, let's give it a whirl!
11th Monkey I'd rather have had a Dodge.

The drums add pace to the scene. The Monkeys equip Rajah with a "body" over which a covering is thrown, mime fitting him with chains, and work starts clearing the timber

4th Assistant In no time at all there were cars to spare—not only in the garages but in the streets, even packed in a permanent traffic-jam at the roundabout outside the village, because, truth to tell, none of the monkeys knew how to drive the things. Nevertheless they were happy. Money was pouring into the village and they felt they were progressing. Only one thing was wrong. They'd reckoned without Rajah.

1st Monkey What's the matter with you? You've only been here a year and already you've lost all your go.

Vedda It's true, you know. You used to be really keen on this job at one time.

Rajah I know, I know. The trouble is it strikes me as a bit of a dead end now. You see, I'm a pachyderm that wants to get on in the world.

2nd Monkey Doing what?

Rajah I don't know. Selling things in a shop maybe.

2nd Monkey A shop?

1st Monkey Well, why not? If it keeps him happy.

4th Assistant So to humour him they took him off the trees and put him in the bazaar selling things.

All the Monkeys set up a bazaar and sell and buy things

Rajah Mangoes two rupees a dozen! Bananas, pomegranates, fresh bamboo shoots!

Vedda What am I supposed to do while you're doing this? I feels a real dope, I can tell you, just hanging about like this.

Rajah You can take care of the small change. I'm not very good with coins.

4th Assistant All went well for six months and then the tell-tale signs set in again. "Hurray," said the monkeys. "Now we'll get back to the trees again!" But not a bit of it.

Rajah I think I want to be a school-teacher now.

Vedda A teacher? What do you know about school teaching?

Rajah I can recognize an equilateral triangle when I see one, can't I?

1st Monkey Oh, well if it keeps him happy.

4th Assistant So they gave him a school.

A "school" is set up. The Monkeys attend noisily

Then he wanted to be a lawyer.

The "school" becomes a "court"

Rajah The trouble as I see it, Your Honour, is that the party of the first part is the same as the party of the second part . . .

4th Assistant But the final straw came after the second year. By now the cars were rusting in the garages and trees had overgrown the traffic jam on the roundabout. "When will he get back to work so we can buy some more unrusty cars?" the monkeys asked. But, no.

Rajah I've decided. I want to be a Buddhist monk.

All Monkeys (*separately*) A Buddhist monk? Now this is really ridiculous! Whoever heard of an elephant . . . ? *etc.*

Vedda Are you sure? But what do you know about being a Buddhist monk?

Rajah I know that all things have their origins in stillness, don't I? And I know that acceptance is the root of life.

1st Monkey Oh, very well, but perhaps after this we can get back to making money.

4th Assistant So Rajah became a Buddhist monk and after a time, so skilful was his teaching, that the monkeys came to accept him as a reincarnation of the Buddha and brought him offerings of flowers and included him in their prayers.

The Dance of the Elephant Buddha: Rajah nods gently during this and accepts the offerings with modesty and gravity

And so penetrating was his mind, so gentle his manner, that soon the monkeys forgot about the cars and washing-machines and making money. They even stopped thinking of themselves as humans and found they were just . . .

10th Monkey Monkeys! That's all we are. Just——

11th Monkey Monkeys!

4th Assistant And were pleased with the thought.

12th Monkey No more keeping up with the Joneses.

They hug and congratulate one another

4th Assistant As for Rajah——

Rajah How strange it is, Lord Buddha. Once I was an elephant who wanted to get on in the world, but now having nothing, I want nothing. In your whole scheme of things I am smaller than the smallest ant, for you have taught me humility and I am content to be only what I am.

4th Assistant So he spent the rest of his days as a teacher of monkeys and is remembered even now as Rajah the Elephant who was always More or Less than what he seemed.

All the Monkeys listen devoutly as silently he expounds his teaching. The Storyteller beckons Vedda and tells him a story

Storyteller Once there was a king who longed to know the ultimate secret of the universe. He sent all his philosophers abroad with this instruction: find me the secret of all things, but in two words. "In two words?" they said. "Surely it cannot be done." "It must be done," he said. "Distill all your learning down to *two words* and bring the answer to me." And then he waited and waited for their return. Perhaps he did not expect them to succeed. Perhaps it was as much a test of them as of their learning. And then one day his favourite philosopher came home. "Have you found it?" he asked anxiously. "Have you found the answer?" "I have found it," the philosopher replied, "I have found the two words you wanted." (*To Vedda*) Do you know what they are?

Vedda No, master.

Storyteller Everything passes. That's all. Everything passes. (*A conspiratorial wink at the audience*) And the king knew he was right. That's what Rajah is telling them now.

Aquila Rubbish. Reactionary bourgeois sentimental rubbish!

A reaction by all

What about the suffering man causes you? Does that pass?

Rajah (*mildly*) Actually he's done me very little harm.

Moja You're lucky. If you'd been born in my country you'd have been hunted for your tusks!

Rajah Surely not!

Moja And not just hunted . . . shot by poisoned arrows, caught in traps, mutilated, allowed to wander in pain and humiliation to die of hunger or gangrene or madness so that they could rip the living tusks from your head and sell them for gold.

Recorder Does that still go on? I thought it had been stopped.

Moja It goes on. Ask the elephants of East Africa if it's been stopped.

Recorder Shameful, scandalous! I positively refuse to write another word.

Some (*separately*) Shameful! Scandalous! . . . *etc.*

Others (*separately*) No, that's one-sided! Let's have the facts! . . . *etc.*

Moja What more facts do you want?

Humming-bird In Canada they club the baby seals to death for their skins.

Aquila Others kill the tiger for his. And the leopard. And the crocodile.

Donkey In Italy they shoot larks and finches for sport . . .

Orca And everybody is dredging the sea for fish!

Uproar! All the Dancers lift their placards and demonstrate on behalf of the species they wish to save

Chamberlain BE SILENT! BE SILENT! BE SILENT! (*He races up to the gong, snatches the stick from the musician and strikes the instrument over and over again until he has restored order*) How can you behave like this in front of the god?

A long pause. All bow down to Tanga including the animals—all that is except Aquila. The Chamberlain looks at him shocked

(*With hatred*) Heretic! (*He covers his head for Tanga*)

Aquila I bow only to *my* god.

Storyteller (*pleasantly but firmly*) Then bow to him.

A pause. The Storyteller and Aquila stare at each other in silence. And then the latter covers his face with his wings

(*Looking round*) Now all living things bow to their god.

A long silence. The Lights slowly return to normal. Order has been restored. They resume their places

Now I think it is time to hear the man-story.

Chamberlain There are others!

Storyteller They can wait. Call the human.

Clerks The human . . . the human . . . the human!

Aquila Now we'll see.

Chamberlain (*to Aquila, nervously*) It will be impartial?

Aquila (*leering*) Of course, of course.

The Human enters. Behind her are three black-robed and hooded figures

The Dancers crowd round the Girl to wish her luck. A great deal of movement until the Chamberlain gives the nod, the Musician strikes the gong and everybody resumes his place

Chamberlain Begin your story.

Human I was born about two thousand million years ago—nobody knows for sure—of a mixture of water, carbon dioxide, ammonia and methane under the influence of sunlight. As a result of the self-replicating system, I passed on my main genetic characteristic by means of a small section of DNA, sometimes mutating, but always growing.

The Lights start to go down. In the background, strange sounds, not quite space-music, are heard

All creatures alive today are probably descended from that same first cell. Under the skin we are all brothers. At first I was probably no bigger than that tiny cell, then a metazoan, then a tadpole, then a fish. Later I probably crawled the earth, grew legs, walked, stood upright. All this took hundreds of millions of years, but the miracle which is God or nature or change kept pushing me on. I did not know my destiny. At the second beginning I was probably a primate, an ape, but smaller, weaker than many of the others of that species. However I had one advantage over the others. I had a better brain.

The animals laugh

Aquila A brain? It didn't do you much good!

Human On the contrary, it saved me. I made up for my lack of inches by using tools. I had advantages—with two eyes in front of my head I had three-dimensional vision, and my digestion could cope with a mixed diet. Fifteen million years ago or so, the forests of our ancestral apes were seriously reduced in size. Where other primates had difficulty in finding food, I struck out on my own—a vegetarian with the instincts of a carnivore.

Moja And that's what you still are! Nothing more, nothing less!

Human But see how successful we became! To survive we had to become better hunters than those who had evolved as carnivores—you, Moja, the tigers and leopards. Our claws were nothing compared with yours, Aquila—but we had to outdo you to live. So we used our skills: our brains, our agility, our eyes and our grasping hands. And we survived.

The Dancers have been following this. Now they are swaying, discovering their hands, their hair, their eyes. Some work in pairs or groups, exploring the earth, scanning the sky, discovering a leaf for the first time. They begin to move—in slow motion—enjoying their freedom in space. The drum accents the rhythm gently, allowing the Human to continue speaking

From tool-using to tool-making. Our hunting methods improved. So did our sense of social co-operation. We hunted in packs, bonded in pairs. We communicated. Planned. We could sense our destiny now.

Humming-bird Arrogant even then!

Human What is survival but arrogance? You at the cost of your neighbours, you at the cost of another species. The master plan is ruthless. We all know that.

Donkey And you talk of being brothers under the skin?

Human But as individuals! As members of a family are individuals!

The Dancers begin hunting. Others remain behind, make fires, care for the young

Now another change came about. We stopped wandering, built home bases—now the hunting ape settled down. Food was brought back to the base, prepared there, stored there. We communicated with our young.
Aquila So do we!
Human But over a longer period. Our complex brains brought disadvantages, taking longer to develop than our bodies. So our young need protection longer than yours. This brought a new form of sub-culture: bonding in family groups.
Aquila Not so new. The Muscovy duck does the same.
Human We do not claim to be unique. Only that in adapting our instincts we have tried to understand them.
Moja Everything you have learnt, you have learnt from us.
Human Not everything.
Moja Everything!

The Dancers break off to listen

Camouflage in your hunting. A flower-spider can change its colour in a week and then change back again. A chameleon can do it in fifteen minutes. Even flat-fish change their colour to match the sea-bed.
Humming-bird Your flying machines copy our principles of flight but you still cannot fly yourselves.
Aquila Your hunting instruments are based on our claws and talons. Even your guns are not new. An archer fish can shoot its prey at fifteen feet.
Orca Dolphins used sound waves long before you did. Bats emit cries in bursts of two hundred a second to find their position. The squid and octopus use jet propulsion. The flying phalanger can glide a hundred yards.
Donkey Termites build towers in which to live which are virtually indestructible. The weaver bird sews his nest with beak and grass. A rattlesnake "sees" with infra-red rays. Bees keep the temperature of the hive cool by standing at the entrance and fanning with their wings——
Human All this is true, but can you *explain* the principles of flight, of jet propulsion, of radar and electrical energy?
Aquila The African knife-fish makes electricity between its head and tail.
Human But does it know what it's doing? In half a million years we have gone from making a fire to making a space-craft. We have stood on the moon, sent vessels even further out into space.
Moja And destroyed life on so monumental a scale, we animals flee at the mere mention of your name.
Human And saved it too!
Donkey One thing you have not conquered—yourselves. Now that your females do not go on heat, they are available to you at any time. So you reproduce and reproduce and now you overpopulate the earth. Even when your females are pregnant——

Humming-bird I've heard of this.

Donkey —you continue this activity. No self-respecting primate would allow this. As for taking a female by force——

Moja There is no rape in the animal world, no crime as you know it.

Human We do not claim we are perfect.

Aquila Yet you set yourselves up as gods!

Human Only the worst of us. The rest know it may take another million years—perhaps more—to knit the two sides of ourselves together. In any struggle to improve, yes, we do fall behind again.

Moja (*triumphant*) So you have not won?

Human No, in many ways we are no better than you.

Aquila (*in a rage*) That's not what he meant! Your animal side is still your better side!

Human No! We believe there is something more. Listen to this——

Philosopher (*lecturing one half of the audience*) In the development of Marxian theory, the concept has been almost entirely focussed on the more rational, larger development——

Astro-physicist (*at the same time lecturing the other half*) Nevertheless all students of physics and mathematics know that since the early nineteen twenties Einstein's Special Relativity Theory—SRT—has been experimentally confirmed——

Human (*interrupting them*) Can you equal that?

Moja We can all make *noises*. I can roar. The ass can bray.

Human This is more than that!

Aquila Is Theodore Eicke here?

Eicke Here.

The Lights slowly go cold. The action stills. Fear creeps in

Aquila You were born in Hamburg in eighteen ninety-two?

Eicke I was.

Aquila You started your career in the Imperial German Army as a paymaster, but by the time you were forty-one you were a colonel in charge of the concentration camp at Dachau?

Eicke I was.

The Dancers set up a low keening

Aquila It is true that at Dachau, under your supervision, the most terrible and inhumane medical experiments were carried out on the prisoners, involving the deliberate infection of syphilis, malaria, typhus, jaundice and gangrene, the dissection of living bodies, surgical mutilations and unnatural bone grafting, the deformation of anatomical processes, seeing if people could live without kidneys, stomachs, livers and so on?

Eicke It is.

Aquila And all this carried out in the name of civilization, contributing to the general deaths in all the camps of twelve million people?

Human (*a cry of despair*) No! There are other things——

An extract from Mozart is heard: an intricate and beautiful piece of music

(*To Aquila*) Could you create that?

Uproar. All protest one way or another. The Storyteller ends it with a gesture

Storyteller The time has come to hear from your fellows.

Chamberlain Yes, who are these three?

1st Black Figure I am the common-cold virus. (*To the animals*) Give me the word and I bring the Human to her knees.

2nd Black Figure I am the rabies virus. There are many like me—cholera, smallpox, perhaps even cancer—but I represent them all for I am almost incurable and what cure there is is usually more terrible than the infection.

Aquila And the third?

3rd Black Figure I am the Nucleus, the very kernel of the living cell. Without me . . . everything else will die. I say to you, spare yourselves this trouble. Kill all but me and everything now on earth will evolve again.

Aquila (*tempted*) Like this?

3rd Black Figure (*a shrug*) Or something . . . similar.

Aquila I say he is right! Let Tuan destroy everything but the Nucleus. Then he can start again!

A shocked silence

All (*at length, separately*) Kill everything? All of us? . . . *etc.*

Moja (*uneasily*) No . . . no I don't agree. I'd rather settle for what I have than take my chance of evolving differently.

Donkey It could be *better*.

Humming-bird (*not so sure*) To start again—over two thousand million years?

They look at one another in doubt

Orca No, I think I'd rather be what I am.

Rajah And what I have become.

Human And I.

All (*separately*) Yes, yes and I.

A long pause as they begin to understand what this means: they must await the verdict

Storyteller So there it is. Of course nothing has been decided, but the situation is clear. They may not be happy with what they are, but they believe they *are* what they *are*. (*To the Chamberlain*) The hearings must go on.

Chamberlain (*to the Court*) Do you wish to hear more?

1st Wise One No, no. Man must be saved, that much is clear.

2nd Wise One Absolutely.

4th Wise One No doubt at all.

Aquila No doubt, old one? What has she proved? Only that time and again she fails.

Human Not always.

Moja Tell us.

The Lights change. The drums start

Human We have heroes, just like you. One such was Yama-Hiko who lived in a country north of here. One day he heard that the Mountain God of Fire was threatening his village. He went to see this god who was called Ontake-San.

Yama-Hiko enters. He wears a hip-long sarong like the other boys but a Japanese scarf round his forehead and he carries a quarterstaff. He kneels and bows low in the Japanese fashion

The Dancers kneel also

Yama-Hiko Hear me, O respected god, spare my village and I'll do anything you tell me.

The god appears on some high point, a fearsome figure in Kabuki mask and robes

Ontake-San I know you humans. You've tried to deceive me like this before.

Yama-Hiko Test me and you'll see I speak the truth.

Ontake-San Very well, we'll see . . .

Human Then he turned the samuarai into a—tree . . . a snake . . . a dog . . . a stone . . .

With each word the actor mimes strongly, using his whole body and sounds to show agony and strain

Ontake-San Not bad. Now let's see if you can become——

Human A crocodile . . . a house . . . a mountain . . . a toad . . .

Yama-Hiko mimes all of these

Ontake-San (*descending*) Very impressive. Now you will become a mule and carry me on your back for the rest of your days. If you do that satisfactorily I shall spare your village.

Yama-Hiko kneels. The god mounts him and Yama carries him round and round the acting area

Human This went on for fifteen years and for all that time the people of Yama-Hiko's village had reason to bless him. Then one day they came to a river. "Cross that," Ontake said. Yama's heart faltered. The river was broad with rushing water so powerful it carried treetrunks before it like matchwood. "Cross it," the god said, "with me on your back or I'll destroy your village."

Yama-Hiko enters the water tentatively, Ontake still clinging to his neck . . .

He reached halfway across and then his foot slipped on a stone! Over they went . . .

They roll over and over. Ontake-San recovers first. He draws his sword

Ontake-San Yama-Hiko, you have failed to carry me and so broken your word. Now I shall kill you and then destroy your village.

Human Then Yama-Hiko knew there was only one thing for it. He had to kill the god before he himself was killed.

The fight starts. Yama with his quarterstaff, Ontake with his sword. It should be as realistic as possible and therefore must be carefully plotted and rehearsed. They fight on all levels, yelling and shouting with each blow. Several times they disappear out of one entrance and re-enter from another. All the Dancers follow at a crouch. If there are galleries in the theatre they cross these too. The struggle is meant to illustrate man's courage and spirit. So each time Yama is knocked to the ground he pulls himself up again. Very soon we realize he is not going to win. He knows that too but keeps going. All the time the drums go and the spectators react: each time he is wounded, they groan. When he stands again, they cheer and exhort him to continue. Even the animals find themselves caught up in admiration. Time after time they cross the stage, leave, re-enter, fall, recover, fall, recover again, fall once more. At length Yama is too injured to continue. He drags himself to his feet, is struck down again, rises, and is struck down again. He tries once more. And dies. Even the god is exhausted. He wipes his sword and sheathes it

Ontake-San Truly this was more than a man. I cannot take his village.

He goes

Human And because of his courage, Yama-Hiko's village was never threatened again.

Enthusiastic applause from all but Aquila. The Lights return to normal

Yama-Hiko picks himself up, takes his bow and runs off

Moja What a fight! I liked that, I really did.

Aquila You like a good fight?

Moja Of course I do. I'm only human, aren't I? (*He realizes what he has said*)

A general laugh—except from Aquila

Well, I say the human has acquitted herself well. Let her go and call the next candidate.

All (*separately*) Yes, let her go. Excellent. Congratulations ... etc. (*They crowd round the Human to thank her*)

A sudden cry of rage from Aquila

Aquila No, this is too easy! How can you thank man for what he has done? (*She swoops down on the Nucleus, knocks him over with her wings and stands threatening him*) Now what will you do? I have the Nucleus!

All react in fear. Cries of fear, of horror

One false move and he'll die.

Nucleus (*terrified*) No, Aquila, no! Kill me and *all* life will die.

More reactions

Aquila Exactly. (*To All*) Well?

Chamberlain What . . . do you want?

Aquila First, the death of man. Second, only the species that I select shall be
allowed to live.

Moja But that is behaving *like* man! How can you make demands like that?

Aquila Man brought violence into the world. Now let him perish by it.

Orca Come, Aquila, that is no way to settle our differences.

Aquila (*raising a threatening claw*) Agree or . . .

The gong strikes. Tangaroa has risen. All except Aquila fall to their knees

Tangaroa The god Tuan speaks through my mouth.

Aquila backs away furiously

He is deeply moved by what he has seen. Too much rests, he sees, one
upon the other—the worm in the soil, the grass, the ox, the leopard, the
man. The fish in the sea, the bird, the thunder, the sun in the sky, the
clouds above our head. The universality of all things—the elephant, the
ass, the eagle, the lion, the stone, the stone that makes a wall, the wall that
makes a house. The mountain stream, the bamboo reed, the gazelle that
drinks, the twigs that are useful to the bird. The nectar sipped by the
humming-bird, the pollen spread from flower to flower, the crop that
grows, the child that grows, the beetle, the monkey, the whale, the
smallest cell, the virus, the anti-virus, the spider's web, the tree, the roots
of the tree, ourselves. All shall be spared, he says. All. For we cannot have
one of these without the other.

He turns and goes

*Huge relief from all. They stay on their knees except the Storyteller who rises
and comes forward*

Storyteller So in the very nick of time, ALL were saved! (*As if there had
been any doubt about it*) What do you think of that! (*A huge smile*)
Sometimes I think this earth is nothing but a gigantic space-ship. Where
are we going? When will we arrive?

*The final music starts. All rise and move as if through a door into an aircraft.
There they take their places for a flight into space. The Lights change*

We have food for the journey—if we are careful. Enough water, clothing,
energy even—again, if we are very, very careful. And time too . . . all the
time in the Universe.

The cast begin to hum the wordless song

Out beyond the moon to the stars. Not drifting in space, but proceeding
purposefully, past quasars and black holes through clouds of helium and
methane and ammonia, past the dead stars further out, carrying with us
our tiniest cells—so small you cannot see them even with a microscope—
to the biggest living species, the world itself. Going on and on and on . . .

The singing grows louder

Proceeding together. The sad, the tawdry and all the splendid things of life. Together. For we are all part of one another, living and dead, young and old, locked in a dream of God who is also inside us and around us. Perhaps in the end the whole of created life will be rescued from the tyranny of fear and have its share in the magnificent freedom which belongs to all His children.

He bows for the last time. The Lights start to fade

(*With a gentle smile*) And if not . . . well, everything passes.

He blows gently at the Lights and they all go out

FURNITURE AND PROPERTY LIST

ACT I

On stage: Block of stone
Gong

Off stage: Drums **(Drummers)**
Finger-bells, clackers **(Dancers)**
Staff **(Chamberlain)**
Palanquin **(Boys)**
Records **(Bookish)**
Lists, scrolls **(Chamberlain's staff)**
Stone and chisel **(Recorder)**
Masks **(Lions)**
Demon mask, spear **(Devil-lion)**
Whale head-piece **(Orca)**
Halter, blindfold for Donkey **(Dancers)**

Personal: **Tangaroa:** mask
Storyteller: golden ball

ACT II

On stage: As before

Off stage: Drums **(Drummers)**
Finger-bells, clackers, placards **(Dancers)**
Cloth for Elephant **(Monkeys)**
Quarterstaff **(Yama-Aiko)**
Sword, Kabuki mask **(Ontake-San)**

LIGHTING PLOT

Property fittings required: *nil*

Exterior. A jungle clearing

BEFORE THE PLAY

To open: General working lighting on stage

Cue 1   When ready   (Page vii)
House and stage lights down

ACT I

To open: Black-out

Cue 2   South of tropical birds   (Page 1)
Bring up lighting on **Storyteller**

Cue 3   **Drummers** begin drumming   (Page 2)
Increase to general lighting

Cue 4   **Cheeky Boy:** "Sing it!"   (Page 4)
Flash of lightning

Cue 5   **Storyteller:** ". . . about to begin"   (Page 6)
Lights narrow down to central area

Cue 6   **1st Assistant:** ". . . by the King Moja." ·   (Page 7)
Increase to very hot, dry lighting

Cue 7   **1st Assistant:** ". . . in search of its blanket." (Page 8)
Fade to night lighting

Cue 8   **Moja:** ". . . I could have sworn——"   (Page 10)
Lightning—continue

Cue 9   **Moja:** ". . . listen to me!"   (Page 10)
Cut lightning

Cue 10   **Devil** scurries off   (Page 12)
Increase to sunny lighting

Cue 11   **All** (*separately*): ". . . what a surprise . . ." *etc.* (Page 14)
Lights up on **Elephant**

Cue 12   **Chamberlain:** "The humming-bird!"   (Page 14)
Lights change

Cue 13   **3rd Assistant:** ". . . speaks for size."   (Page 18)
Lights become green, with ripple effect

Cue 14   **Storyteller:** "... strongest points lie."   (Page 22)
          Return to general lighting

Cue 15   **Clerks:** "Adjourned ... adjourned!"   (Page 26)
          Fade lights to spot on **Storyteller**

Cue 16   **Storyteller** looks up at spot and gives a gentle puff   (Page 26)
          Cut spot to black-out

ACT II

To open: General working lighting on stage

Cue 17   **Storyteller** nods to **Drummers**, bows to audience; drums break   (Page 27)
          off
          Fade house and stage lights; bring up spot on **Aquila**

Cue 18   **Aquila** stretches her wings   (Page 27)
          Increase to general lighting

Cue 19   **Aquila:** "Then, listen."   (Page 28)
          Fade to spot on **Aquila**

Cue 20   **Aquila:** "... a chance to move."   (Page 29)
          Increase to general lighting

Cue 21   **Aquila:** "... curse them!"   (Page 30)
          Fade to spot on **Storyteller**

Cue 22   **Storyteller:** "But first——"   (Page 30)
          Increase to general lighting

Cue 23   **3rd Wise One:** "... on his two feet."   (Page 31)
          Fade lights to **4th Assistant**

Cue 24   **Dancers** scatter as monkeys   (Page 31)
          Shafts of light as though through foliage in jungle

Cue 25   **Storyteller:** "... to their god."   (Page 35)
          Slowly return to general lighting

Cue 26   **Human:** "... but always growing."   (Page 36)
          Slowly fade lighting

Cue 27   **Eike:** "Here."   (Page 38)
          Lights slowly go cold

Cue 28   **Moja:** "Tell us."   (Page 39)
          Lights change

Cue 29   Enthusiastic applause from all but **Aquila**   (Page 41)
          Return to general lighting

Cue 30   **All** take their places for a flight into space   (Page 42)
          Lights change

Cue 31   **Storyteller:** "... all his children."   (Page 43)
          Lights start to fade

Cue 32   **Storyteller** blows gently at the lights   (Page 43)
          Black-out

EFFECTS PLOT

BEFORE THE PLAY

Cue 1   Ten minutes before curtain-up   (Page vii)
         Sound of orchestra tuning up, plus murmur and excitement of a
         large and expectant audience

Cue 2   Fifteen minutes before curtain-up   (Page vii)
         Orchestra sounds become louder

Cue 3   M-Minute   (Page vii)
         Cut orchestra; pause, then loud applause

ACT I

Cue 4   After house lights have gone down   (Page 1)
         5 big crashes on oriental drum; then sound of tropical birds
         shrieking, calling, chattering

Cue 5   **Storyteller:** "Be quiet ... *please.*"   (Page 1)
         Cut bird noise

Cue 6   **Drummers** start drumming   (Page 2)
         Bring up bird noise

Cue 7   **Chamberlain** commands silence   (Page 3)
         Cut bird noise

Cue 8   **Cheeky Boy:** "Sing it!"   (Page 4)
         Crash of thunder

Cue 9   **Moja:** "... cumulo-nimbus anywhere."   (Page 10)
         Distant growl of thunder

Cue 10   **Moja:** "... I could have sworn——"   (Page 10)
         Giant crack of thunder, rain—continue

Cue 11   **Moja:** "... listen to me!"   (Page 10)
         Cut storm sounds

Cue 12   As **Voice** laughs   (Page 11)
         Echo in rumbles of thunder

Cue 13   **Moja:** "... see your face."   (Page 11)
         Thunder. Face of devil projected on gauze or smoke

Cue 14   **All** (*separately*): "Yes, yes, come down here ..." *etc.*   (Page 12)
         Wind and thunder return to a crescendo, then break off

Cue 15   **Moja:** "... you hear the sound ..."   (Page 12)
         Amplified lions' roaring

Cue 16   **3rd Assistant:** "... He speaks for size."   (Page 18)
         Heavy waves breaking, sea-birds, then series of shrill, piping
         notes

Cue 17   **Orca:** "... sport and roll."   (Page 19)
         Whales' song

Cue 18   As cast cry out name of species   (Page 22)
         Giant trumpetting, roaring, chirping, twittering off-stage

Cue 19   **Chamberlain:** "... will be selected."   (Page 22)
         Gradually fade off-stage noises

ACT II

Cue 20   **Aquila:** "Liar. Liar. Liar."   (Page 28)
         Screaming of eagles

Cue 21   **Aquila:** "... you've taken everything!"   (Page 30)
         Screaming of eagles

Cue 22   **Aquila:** "... curse them!"   (Page 30)
         Fade eagles

Cue 23   **Dancers** scatter as monkeys   (Page 31)
         Tropical noises

Cue 24   **Human:** "... but always growing."   (Page 36)
         Strange sounds, not quite space-music, in background

Cue 25   **Human** "... other things——"   (Page 38)
         Extract from Mozart

MADE AND PRINTED IN GREAT BRITAIN BY
LATIMER TREND & COMPANY LTD PLYMOUTH
MADE IN ENGLAND

Lightning Source UK Ltd.
Milton Keynes UK
UKHW022241070220
358378UK00006B/484